LIVING IN
ASIA

Living in
CHINA

Annabelle Lynch

W
FRANKLIN WATTS
LONDON•SYDNEY

Franklin Watts
First published in Great Britain in 2016 by The Watts Publishing Group

Credits
Series Editor: Julia Bird
Series Design: D.R. ink

ISBN 978 1 4451 4859 5

Picture credits: aphotostory/Shutterstock: 19c, 23t. Juan Camilo Bernal/Shutterstock: 5b. Stephane Bidouze/Shutterstock: 7cb. Hung Chung Chih/Shutterstock: 11b, 18b, 22b. cloud7days/Shutterstock: 14b. Delpixel/Shutterstock: 21b. Design Pics Inc/Alamy: 18c. T Dway/Shutterstock: 19b. Elwynn /Shutterstock: 8b. farbled/Shutterstock: 15t. Hanoi Photography/Shutterstock: 8t. John Henshall/Alamy: 16b, 20b. Jiang Hongyan/Shutterstock: 8c, 21c. Guangliang Huo/Dreamstime: 21t. imtmphoto/Shutterstock: 6t. Su Jianfei/Shutterstock: 7c. Jpidesigns/Dreamstime: 15b. konglingnang/istockphoto: 17t. Lalkwuhfai/istockphoto: 16t. leungchopan/Shutterstock: 13b. fuyu liu/Shutterstock: 20c. mamahoohooba/Shutterstock: 4t. Martial Red/Shutterstock: 7b. Max Studio/Shutterstock: 19t. Nithid/Shutterstock: 7t. nui7711/Shutterstock: front cover. Sean Pavone/Shutterstock: 10b. maoyun ping/Shutterstock: 11t. Qin0377/Dreamstime: 5t. Rawpixel.com/Shutterstock: 12t. Evgeny Ryazanov/Dreamstime: 12b. Sanmongkhol/Shutterstock: 18t. Sushaaa/Dreamstime: 13t. szefei/Shutterstock: 20t. testing/Shutterstock: 6b. TonyV3112/Shutterstock: 9b. Vogel/Shutterstock: 11c. James Wheeler/Shutterstock: 9t. Xi Xin Xing/Shutterstock: 14t. wong sze yuen/Shutterstock: 10t. claudio zaccherini/Shutterstock: 17b.

Printed in Malaysia

Franklin Watts
An imprint of
Hachette Children's Group
Part of The Watts Publishing Group
Carmelite House
50 Victoria Embankment
London EC4Y 0DZ

An Hachette UK Company
www.hachette.co.uk

www.franklinwatts.co.uk

Contents

Words in bold are in the glossary on page 23.

Welcome to China!

Ni hao! Hello!
Welcome to China.

Where is China?

China is found in East Asia. It is the fourth largest country in the world, after Russia, Canada and the USA. China stretches for over nine million square kilometres across Asia. It has **borders** with fourteen other countries and a long **coastline** along the Pacific Ocean.

The Yellow River flows across China.

What does China look like?

China is so big that its **landscape** is very varied. It has snowy mountains, scorching **deserts** and wide, flat grasslands. Two huge rivers flow across China, the Yellow River to the north and the Yangtze to the south.

What's the weather like?

The **climate** in China is different depending on where you are. In the north, the summers are dry and winters are very cold. In the central area, there is more rain all year round. To the south, the summers are hot and **humid**, and winters are shorter and warmer.

People in China

I come from China. People from China are called Chinese.

Lots of people

China has the largest **population** in the world, with over 1.35 billion people. Around one in five people living in the world today is Chinese! Over the years, Chinese people have settled in other countries around the world, including the USA, the UK and Australia.

A crowded street in Shenzhen, China

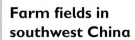

The Gobi Desert in northern China

Farm fields in southwest China

Where people live

Most people in China live in the east of the country where there are big cities to work in or **fertile** land to farm. Far fewer people live in the mountains or the desert areas in the west and north of China.

Burning incense in a Buddhist temple

Religion

Many people in China follow **traditional** Chinese religions, such as Taoism. Others follow the teachings of Buddhism, while some are Christian or Muslim. Many people follow no religion at all.

Taoism

Tao means 'the way'. Its followers believe in the balance of everything in the world. Its symbol is the yin and yang (left).

Country life

Over half of China's population still lives in or near towns and villages in the countryside. I live in a village in the south of China.

On the farm

Most people in the countryside make a living from farming. China has over 300 million farmers and produces enough food for a fifth of the world's population. Other country jobs include forestry and building projects.

rice field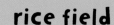

soya beans

China's top crops include rice, wheat, potatoes, peanuts, tea, tomatoes and soya beans.

A quieter life

Most people in the countryside live in two or three-storey houses. Some **remote** villages are difficult to get to because of poor roads or transport links. Most homes have electricity and running water, but some still do not. Village **communities** are very important and people have close relationships with their neighbours.

Move to the city

In recent years, many millions of people have moved from the countryside to the cities, where they often live in blocks of flats. People can earn more money in the city. There are more jobs too, and a wider variety available.

Cities

China has many big cities. I live in the bustling city of Shanghai.

Watery place

Shanghai is the biggest city in China. It is found on China's east coast, next to the East China Sea and close to the mouth of the great Yangtze River. Its location near the sea and the Yangtze have made Shanghai one of the most important **ports** in the world.

The Shanghai skyline

Shopping in Wangfujing, Beijing

Beautiful Beijing

Beijing is China's **capital** city and its second biggest city. It has a rich history and millions of **tourists** come here every year to visit places such as the Forbidden City and the Great Wall of China (see page 18). Beijing is found in northeast China.

Shopping in Wangfujing, Beijing

Panda city

The city of Chengdu is found in southwest China, where the land is mostly flat and fertile. There are few other big cities in this part of China, so people come from a long way away to find work here. Tourists also come here to visit the famous giant panda **nature reserve**.

giant pandas

China's top five cities by population

Shanghai: 23 million
Beijing: 20 million
Tianjin: 13 million
Guangzhou: 12 million
Shenzhen: 10 million

Wildlife

I live on a farm and we have horses. China is home to some wonderful and rare wildlife, some of which cannot be found anywhere else in the world.

Snap snap!

The rare Chinese alligator is one of the smallest **crocodilians**. It hunts at night and feeds mostly on fish and shellfish. It once lived on the banks of the Yangtze in eastern China, but now is only found in nature reserves.

Chinese alligator

clouded leopard

Spotty cats

Clouded leopards are found in the warm, thick forests of southern China. They are great hunters who spend much of their life up trees and can do amazing stunts, including hanging upside down from branches!

China has some really unusual animals, including jumping mice and flying squirrels!

Giant pandas

Giant pandas are found in the cool forests of western China, where they munch on bamboo all day long. Over the years, the number of pandas has got smaller as the bamboo forests where they live have been cut down for wood or to build homes. There are around 1,600 giant pandas left in the wild, but China is now working to protect their **habitat**.

What we eat

We enjoy food cooked in lots of different ways in China. What we eat often depends on what people can buy locally.

Tea was first drunk in China thousands of years ago, and is now grown all over the country. Chinese people never add milk or sugar to their tea!

Chop chop

People don't use a knife and fork to eat in China. Instead, they use a pair of thin sticks, called chopsticks. They can be tricky until you get used to them!

wok

Rice and noodles

In the south of China, where there are lots of rice farms, rice is a big part of people's **diet**. In the north, where wheat is grown, people eat more foods made from wheat, such as noodles. They cook both rice and noodles with lots of vegetables and **soy sauce** in sizzling hot pans called woks. Delicious!

dim sum

Famous dishes

Some Chinese dishes can be enjoyed all over the world, such as *dim sum*. These are bite-sized pieces of food, such as dumplings and buns filled with meat, which are served in steamer baskets. Sweet, crispy duck served in pancakes, known as Peking duck, is also very popular.

Having fun

We love *playing games and spending time outdoors in China.*

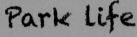 jianzi

Park life

Chinese people love going to the park and we play all sorts of games there, from kite-flying to board games. One popular Chinese park game is called *jianzi*. You have to keep a shuttlecock in the air using any part of your body but your hands!

kung fu

Kung fu

Many types of **martial art** come from China, one popular type is called *kung fu*. Today, there are martial arts schools all over China, where people can learn how to fight with style and control.

Many Chinese people enjoy a traditional game called mah jong. It is played with different coloured tiles and can get very noisy!

Table tennis

Table tennis is one of the most popular sports in China, and people play on tables at home, in schools and in parks. Basketball and football are also popular sports.

Famous places

China has many amazing places to visit. People come from all over the world to see China's top attractions.

Walk the wall

The Great Wall of China is one of the most famous places in the world. People began building it over 2,000 years ago to protect China from attack. Today, the Wall stretches for over 20,000 km across China, although many parts are only **ruins**. At Mutianyu, north of Beijing, you can take a cablecar up part of the wall and slide back down again!

giant slide

Summer Palace

Discover China's past in Beijing's Summer Palace – a huge park made up of palaces, temples and bridges, all surrounding Kunming Lake. You can rent your own boat and cruise around the lake, enjoying the view.

River ride

Take a boat ride or cycle along the Li River near Guilin to explore one of China's most beautiful landscapes, including the famous mountains that rise up from the river valley. Make sure you visit the Reed Flute Cave for an amazing light show.

Festivals

In China we celebrate many traditional festivals throughout the year.

Happy New Year!

In January or February each year, people celebrate Chinese New Year. This is a very special time for all Chinese people. They visit family, eat traditional foods, set off **firecrackers** and watch fireworks. They also give gifts of money called *lai* see in red envelopes to young and old people.

lai see

Boat day

The exciting Dragon Boat Festival is held in May or June every year to remember a famous Chinese poet who drowned. People hold races in special boats that look like dragons. It is great, splashy fun!

In China, people believe that each year is associated with one of twelve different animals. Every Chinese New Year, the animal changes. Which animal is linked to the year of your birth?

2019 Pig
2018 Dog
2017 Rooster
2016 Monkey
2015 Goat
2014 Horse
2013 Snake
2012 Dragon
2011 Rabbit
2010 Tiger
2009 Ox
2008 Rat

moon cakes

Moon gazing

In autumn in China, people celebrate the Mid-Autumn or Moon Festival. They head outdoors to look at the full moon and eat special foods, such as sweet, round mooncakes.

China: Fast facts

Capital: Beijing

Population: 1.357 billion (2013)

Area: 9,597 million sq km

Languages: Mandarin Chinese (official) and many other Chinese languages

Currency: Renminbi

Main religions: Buddhism, Taoism, Confucianism, Islam, Christianity

Longest river: Yangtze, 6,300 km

Highest mountain: Mount Everest, 8,850 m

National holidays: New Year's Day (1 January), Chinese New Year, Qingming (4 or 5 April), May Day (1 May), Dragon Boat Festival, Mid-Autumn Festival (also called the Moon Festival), National Day (1 October)

Glossary

border a line marking the boundary between two countries

capital the city where the country's government meets

climate the regular weather pattern in a region

coastline the line where the land meets the sea

community a group of people living in the same area

crocodilians large reptiles such as crocodiles or alligators

desert a large area of land where there is very little rain

diet the type of food that people usually eat

fertile good for growing crops

firecracker a loud, explosive firework; a banger

habitat where an animal lives in the wild

humid damp

landscape the natural scenery

martial arts fighting sports

nature reserve a protected area for wildlife

population all the people living in a country or area

port a place next to water, from where ships arrive and depart

remote far away from places where other people live

ruins the parts of a building that are left when the rest has fallen down or been destroyed

soy sauce a brown, salty sauce made from soya beans

tourist someone who visits a place on holiday

traditional describes things that have been done in the same way for a long time

Index